C0-CFH-974

IRELAND

The Land of a Hundred Thousand Welcomes

Clare Gallagher

IRELAND: The Land of a Hundred Thousand Welcomes

Text compiled by Clare Gallagher

Summersdale Publishers Ltd
46 West Street
Chichester
West Sussex
PO19 1RP
UK

www.summersdale.com

Printed and bound in the Czech Republic

ISBN: 978-1-84953-520-5

TO ....

FROM ....

CÉAD MÍLE FÁILTE

(Kay-d Meal-a Fawl-tja)
A Hundred Thousand Welcomes

INTRODUCTION

Ireland is a place of unforgettable beauty – verdant hillsides, wending rivers, majestic castles, quaint seaside villages and bustling cities. An air of myth and legend pervades the land; and tales of giants, magical beasts and noble heroes resonate through the country's folk history. The nation has a heart for song and dance, food and drink – the much-sought-after *craic*. It's that special something in the Irish people however – their hospitality, wit and charm – that makes the country what it really is. Many a happy pub-goer will have seen a sign bearing the warm message '*Céad Míle Fáilte*', which in English means 'A Hundred Thousand Welcomes'. This phrase embodies the spirit of Irish hospitality and cheer.

This book raises a glass to all that is best about Ireland, the Land of a Hundred Thousand Welcomes!

FESTIVALS

Festivals have long been a part of the Irish cultural calendar, the most famous of all of course being St Patrick's Day Festival on 17 March every year. Music, theatre and the arts are celebrated all across the island all year round. A selection of the most famous are the Galway Arts Festival, Kilkenny Arts Festival and the Belfast Festival; Cork Film Festival and Galway Film Fleadh; Dublin Theatre Festival; Cork Jazz Festival and Wexford Festival Opera. Those out to excite the taste buds are also catered for at festivals such as the Galway Oyster Festival, the Bantry Mussel Fair and the Irish Craft Beer and Cider Festival.

There are only two kinds
of people in the world,
the Irish and those
who wish they were.

ANONYMOUS

COUNTY DONEGAL

Glenveagh *(Glen-vay)* National Park in County Donegal is a place to truly get away from it all. The 24,000-acre park is an oasis of wilderness comprising mountains, moorland, lakes, forests and a dense undergrowth of russet-coloured heath. The Derryveagh Mountains border the national park and overlook the Irish-speaking coastal area of Gweedore where Irish culture and tradition are very much alive. Near Gweedore stands Donegal's tallest peak, Mount Errigal – the mountain is 2,464 feet high and part of the mountain chain known to locals as the Seven Sisters.

THE CHESTER BEATTY LIBRARY

The Chester Beatty Library in the gardens of Dublin Castle houses a spectacular and fascinating collection of items ranging from ancient illuminated manuscripts and Old Master prints to rare books and decorative arts. Artefacts hail from Asia, the Middle East, North Africa and Europe, and are the result of Sir Alfred Chester Beatty's lifelong love of collecting. Originally born in New York, he made a fortune in copper mines in Colorado and became known as the King of Copper. He travelled widely during his lifetime and in 1950 moved to Ireland where, upon his death, he generously left his collection to a trust for the public's benefit.

A good laugh and a long sleep are the two best cures.

PROVERB

BOA ISLAND

A stroll around spooky Caldragh graveyard on Boa Island, Lough Erne, County Fermanagh might bring you face-to-face with two enigmatic stone statues. The idols are thought to have been carved in the Iron Age (500 BCE–400 CE) in the likeness of pagan deities – one was found in the graveyard and the other brought from nearby Lustymore Island. The Boa Island figure is larger and consists of two busts back-to-back in the fashion of the twin-headed Roman god Janus. According to Celtic beliefs, a person's spirit resides in their head after death, which may explain the emphasis of the statue. The island's name is derived from Badbh *(Baave)* – meaning 'crow' – the goddess of war, who is depicted as a crow or at times a wolf.

IRISH MYTHOLOGY

The plentiful myths and legends of Ireland can broadly be divided into four major cycles of literary tradition. The Mythological Cycle recounts the legends surrounding the gods who arrived in five migratory invasions during the pagan period in Ireland's history. The Ulster Cycle tells of medieval heroic legends and sagas relating to births, battles, feasts and death in the regions of eastern Ulster and northern Leinster, then known as Ulaid. Thirdly, set around the third century CE, the Fenian Cycle, is centred around the heroic adventures of Fionn mac Cumhaill *(Fee-yon mac Kuwal)* or Finn McCool in English, and his warriors the Fianna *(Fee-anna)*. Finally, the Historical Cycle relates to the legendary kings of Ireland.

Some cause happiness wherever they go; others whenever they go.

OSCAR WILDE

LOUGH NEAGH

Sitting in the centre of Ulster is Lough Neagh *(Nay)*, the largest freshwater lake in the whole of Ireland and the United Kingdom. It supplies 40 per cent of Ireland's water, and – in legend, at least – was created when Fionn mac Cumhaill was chasing a Scottish giant across Ireland. Fionn scooped up a large piece of earth, hurled it at the giant and missed, which, in the process, created the Isle of Man. The lough covers 151 square miles and is as deep as 80 feet and connects to the sea via the River Bann. Cycling enthusiasts regularly enjoy the Loughshore Trail that encircles the lake.

THE BLARNEY STONE

Over 200,000 people from all over the world literally bend over backwards to kiss the Blarney Stone every year, in the hope of being bestowed with the 'gift of the gab' or charm. Legend has it that Cormac Laidir (*Law-jer*, meaning 'strong') MacCarthy who built Blarney Castle sought help from the Celtic goddess Clíodhna *(Cliona)* when faced with a court case. Clíodhna instructed Cormac that on the way to court he was to kiss the first stone he came across; kissing the stone caused him to speak with great eloquence in court and win his case.

Lose an hour in the morning and you'll be looking for it all day.

PROVERB

NEWGRANGE

Around the winter solstice, in late December, people flock to Newgrange in County Meath to witness a very special event at the Neolithic monument that is found there. The circular mound was built more than 5,000 years ago and incorporates a 64-foot-long stone passageway and several chambers. Almost 100 curb stones surround the mound, many of them engraved with Neolithic art. At around 9 a.m. on the mornings of the shortest days of the year sunlight illuminates a chamber at the end of the passageway, suggesting some careful consideration went into constructing Newgrange to align it with sunrise in ancient times.

NATIONAL MUSEUM OF IRELAND

The archaeology branch of the National Museum of Ireland houses a fascinating collection of artefacts from prehistoric Ireland through to the Middle Ages and beyond. Highlights include world-renowned examples of medieval Celtic metalwork, such as the exquisite Tara Brooch, the Ardagh Chalice and the Derrynaflan Chalice, dating from around 700–900 CE. They are found in a beautiful Victorian Palladian-style building on Kildare Street in Dublin that opened to the public in 1890. The National Museum of Ireland has three other branches: the Decorative Arts and History Museum and the Natural History Museum in Dublin, and the Country Life Museum in County Mayo.

IS MINIC A BHRIS BEÁL DUINE A SHRÓN.

(Iss minik a vriss bale dine a hrone.)
It is often that a person's
mouth broke his nose.

ADARE

Often referred to as 'Ireland's prettiest village', a trip to the postcard-perfect village of Adare, County Limerick, will make you feel like you've taken a step back in time. Set on the banks of the River Maigue, the village is dotted with perfectly preserved thatch-roof cottages built in the nineteenth century for workers constructing Adare Manor. Nowadays the thatched cottages are home to fine restaurants and craft shops. There are remains of Adare's three religious houses – a church, a priory and a friary – to explore in the village, along with a heritage centre, a castle and a prestigious golf course.

HOWTH PENINSULA

One of Dublin's many seaside villages worth exploring is Howth. To take everything in and work up a good appetite it's best to take a bus from the city centre to Howth summit, where you can experience the spectacular cliff walk. The 5-mile trail winds around the headland affording beautiful sea views – the Wicklow Mountains can be seen to the south and the Mourne Mountains to the north. Arriving into this fishing village, one may come across the ruins of St Mary's Abbey, trawlers laden with the morning's catch, delicious fish shops, pubs and restaurants and a pier for a gentle stroll after enjoying a bite.

May the roof above
you never fall in, and
those gathered beneath
it never fall out.

TRADITIONAL IRISH TOAST

DUBLIN WRITERS MUSEUM

To celebrate Dublin and Ireland's rich literary heritage the Dublin Writers Museum was established in 1991. A beautifully restored Georgian mansion on Parnell Square is home to the intriguing collection of letters, books, personal items and portraits of well-known Irish literary figures such as Samuel Beckett, Oscar Wilde, Mary Lavin and Lady Gregory. The museum also houses a specialist bookshop, temporary exhibitions and lunchtime theatre. The curious collection of personal items – including Beckett's telephone, Lady Gregory's lorgnette and even Lavin's teddy bear – allows visitors to get to know the people behind the books that little bit better.

THE IRISH LANGUAGE

Irish, known as Gaelige *(Gwail-ege)* in the mother tongue, is a Celtic language similar to Manx and Scottish Gaelic although spelling and pronunciation are quite different. In fact, in Ireland alone there are three main dialects that differ significantly: Munster in the south, Connacht in the west and Ulster in the north. The language first appeared in the fourth century using the Ogham alphabet, the oldest system of writing in Ireland, examples of which are mainly found in the south. You can find Modern Irish on street signs around the country; it is the first official language of Ireland, an official language of the EU since 2007, and a minority language in Northern Ireland.

In Ireland the inevitable
never happens and
the unexpected
constantly occurs.

SIR JOHN PENTLAND MAHAFFY

WATERFORD CRYSTAL

The Waterford Glass factory originally opened in 1783 to produce high-end chandeliers, decorative ornaments and handcrafted stemware. The brand is synonymous around the world with top-quality craftwork and beauty. Almost two dozen pairs of hands help fashion each piece of glass before final inspections are passed and the Waterford trademark placed on the piece. Sadly, the factory fell on hard times and closed in 2009. A smaller facility reopened in 2010 where visitors can enjoy a fascinating factory tour taking them through all the production stages from moulding to cutting.

CLIFFS OF MOHER

One of County Clare's highlights is the awesome 5-mile stretch of coast where the entirely vertical Cliffs of Moher reach heights of 710 feet. Sacred in Celtic times and favoured as a hunting spot by the High King of Ireland Brian Boru, the cliffs are breathtaking to behold. A look over the edge at the sheer drop to the swirling sea below is enough to turn the strongest of stomachs, yet it is impossible to turn away from the striking view. The cliffs can also be explored from below on a boat tour, or on rainy days at the visitor centre and interactive exhibition.

The older the fiddle,
the sweeter the tune.

PROVERB

BELFAST CITY HALL

Belfast's Renaissance Revival-style City Hall was built between 1898 and 1906 and modelled on St Paul's Cathedral in London. Located in Donegall Square, in the heart of the city centre, the building is surrounded by ample gardens, statues and monuments. The elaborate interior includes Belfast's most ornate public space, the 173-foot high Great Dome, as well as a whispering gallery, wall mural and grand staircase. On special occasions the building is lit up in a variety of colours and designs to highlight its majestic architectural features.

FIONN MAC CUMHAILL

Fionn mac Cumhaill is one of the most famous characters of Irish mythology featuring in the Fenian Cycle of literature. Fionn means 'blond' or 'white' and it seems the warrior earned this nickname when his hair was said to have turned prematurely white. One legend tells how he met his most famous wife, Sadbh *(Sigh-ve)*, out hunting. After refusing to marry a druid, Sadbh was turned into a deer; yet Fionn's hounds knew Sadbh was human as they had once been men, and so Fionn let her live. Upon setting foot on Fionn's land Sadbh became a woman again and they married. However, the legend also explains that she was later turned back into a deer and then vanished. Fionn spent seven unhappy years looking for her to no avail.

Ireland is rich in literature
that understands a soul's
yearnings, and dancing that
understands a happy heart.

MARGARET JACKSON

THE HILL OF TARA

As the seat of the high kings of Ireland until the eleventh century, the Hill of Tara was a place where tribal disputes were settled and laws were passed. It lies at the junction of the five ancient roads of Ireland, in the Boyne Valley, Meath. While the ancient buildings and banqueting halls have been reduced to a few columns, the legends surrounding the area live on. Standing 300 feet above sea level, visitors to the Hill of Tara can see far across the flat central plain of Ireland as far as 100 miles away to the mountains of eastern Galway.

ULSTER AMERICAN FOLK PARK

To see how the people of Ulster and America lived a couple of centuries back, one can spend a day exploring the Ulster American Folk Park in County Tyrone. It tells the story of the hundreds of thousands who emigrated to America in the eighteenth and nineteenth centuries and the close connections between both places. Wander around a typical Ulster village, blacksmith's forge and weaver's thatched cottage where staff dress in period costumes. Explore an original eighteenth-century, log-built American settlement (shipped 2,900 miles across the Atlantic) and the docks and ships that would have been used by emigrants to America. Celebrations of Irish and American culture take place throughout the year.

Better good manners
than good looks.

PROVERB

KILKENNY CASTLE

Built in 1172 and home to one of Ireland's most powerful clans for over 500 years from 1391, Kilkenny Castle is an historic gem. It combines Gothic and Victorian styles, is set next to the River Nore and surrounded by 50 acres of rolling lawn. The ornate interior houses family portraits, Celtic lacework, tapestries and animal heads as well as an excellent collection of Irish modern art in the former servants' quarters. Kilkenny City, referred to as Ireland's medieval capital, is both a picturesque town full of historic sites and a lively nightspot that's popular for weekend jaunts.

THE GAELTACHT

For those curious about the Irish language, the Gaeltacht *(Gwail-tockt)* or Irish-speaking regions are populated by over 100,000 people. For a significant number of these people, Irish is the main spoken language for their day-to-day activities and among family. The regions can be found in parts of west coast counties Donegal, Mayo, Galway and Kerry as well as in Cork, Meath and Waterford and on six offshore islands. Traditionally spoken more in rural areas, the Irish language underwent a revival in cities such as Dublin and Belfast during the late twentieth century where Irish cultural centres were established and many more Gaelscoileanna *(Gwail-skull-anna)* or Irish schools opened where all subjects are taught through the Irish language.

NÍL AON TINTEÁN MAR DO THINTEÁN FÉIN.

(Neel ayne tin-tawn mar du hin-tawn fayne.)
There is no fireside like your own fireside.

CORK CITY

The second city of the Republic, Cork City is referred to by locals as 'the real capital of Ireland'. The city's name comes from the Irish word Corkaigh *(Kirk-ig)* meaning 'marshy place'. The initial settlement was spread over thirteen small islands on the River Lee where a monastery was established in the sixth century. The city's many waterways, bridges and quays lend it much character, while also making navigation a little confusing at times. Grand Georgian architecture combines with narrow winding streets, making for a pleasant ramble to uncover many great restaurants and a vibrant arts and entertainment scene.

CLADDAGH RINGS

The Claddagh *(Clad-ah)* area of Galway started producing its world-famous rings in the seventeenth century. Handcrafted in silver and gold, the ring design comprises a heart, symbolising love, naturally, held between two outstretched hands, representing friendship, and a crown on top for loyalty. The rings are worn by singles and couples in Ireland and around the world to signal their relationship status: if worn on the right hand with the crown and heart facing upright, it indicates the wearer's heart has yet to be captured. If the heart and crown face downwards, the wearer is romantically involved but not yet married. On the left hand an upright ring means engagement and downwards, marriage.

All the world's a stage
and most of us are
desperately unrehearsed.

SEAN O'CASEY

MEAT AND DAIRY

Ireland's green pastures are more than just pleasing to the eye, they are home to around 140,000 family farms that form a major part of the Irish economy. Traditional farming methods such as grass-feeding mean Irish beef and lamb are prized the world over for their texture and flavour. The importance of meat and dairy is highlighted in Irish folklore too, where in the Cattle Raid of Cooley Queen Maeve leads a war to steal a famously fertile bull from Ulster. Historically people believed that witches or fairies would 'steal the profit' from world-renowned Irish butter. Cheesemaking has also been refined to an art and many farmhouse cheeses including Cashel Blue, Coolea and Durrus are celebrated at home and abroad.

THE IVEAGH GARDENS

To get away from the hustle and bustle of Dublin city centre, locals like to take their lunches and books to the Iveagh *(Ivy)* Gardens, a quiet, leafy spot hidden away behind the National Concert Hall. Designed in 1865, the walled gardens were an intermediate design between the 'English landscape' and 'French formal' styles. A stroll around will take you from the sweet scent of the circular rose garden to finding your way around the miniature maze. A perfectly manicured lawn with fountain centre pieces also feature, as does a rustic grotto and cascade, along with American gardens, rockeries and archery grounds.

We don't stop playing
because we grow old;
we grow old because
we stop playing.

GEORGE BERNARD SHAW

THE LEGEND OF TÍR NA NÓG

Tír na nÓg *(Tear nah nogue)* is a mythical 'land of the young', located on an island far to the west of the mainland. The land of eternal youth and beauty, it was believed to be a paradise where there is no sickness or death, only happiness, music, life and pleasure. Inhabited by supernatural beings, visitors must be invited by one of the island's fairy residents or undertake an arduous voyage to make it there. The isle features in many popular Irish myths, particularly the *immram*- (voyage) and *echtrae*- (adventure) style tales from the Middle Ages.

THE SKELLIG ROCKS

Off the western shores of the Iveragh *(I-vur-ah)* Peninsula lie the Skellig *(Shkellig)* Rocks. The two islands, Little Skellig and Great Skellig (or Skellig Michael) have a distinctive conical form and are a birdwatcher's paradise. Despite appearing inhospitable, Skellig Michael, a UNESCO World Heritage Site, was home to Christian monks between the sixth and thirteenth centuries. The remains of the monastery, including beehive cells and a church, are perched on a ledge and can be reached by climbing 600 steep steps cut into the rock face. The island is also distinguished by two peaks, the higher of the two reaching 700 feet.

May misfortune follow
you the rest of your life,
and never catch up.

TRADITIONAL IRISH TOAST

SLIEVE BLOOM

Another midlands highlight is the peaceful Slieve *(shleeve)* Bloom mountain range that connects counties Offaly and Laois. The necklace of quaint villages that surround the range are pleasant starting places for looped trails ranging from 3 to 12 miles long. The mountains themselves, along with their twenty-seven glens, are awash with lush forests, waterfalls and freshwater streams and providing idyllic surroundings for those wanting a gentle stroll and a more serious hike. The views are spectacular and on a clear day the high points of all the ancient provinces are visible.

IRISH CUISINE

Irish cuisine is necessarily hearty considering the weather, and heavily influenced by the humble potato, a nutritious discovery brought to Ireland in 1589 by Sir Walter Raleigh. The potato enabled tenant farmers to subsist where soil was poor, as the best land was used to grow barley for export. A few examples of classic dishes are colcannon – mashed potato mixed with kale or cabbage and butter; coddle – braised sliced pork sausages, back bacon, potatoes, onions and barley in stock; and boxty – a pancake made of grated and mashed potato. Irish stew is another winter warmer consisting of lamb, potatoes, onions, carrots and parsley. Homemade Irish brown bread – each household's recipe slightly different – is the perfect accompaniment to hot soup on a winter's day.

There is no language like
the Irish for soothing
and quieting.

JOHN MILLINGTON SYNGE

THE *TITANIC* TRAIL

The *Titanic* Trail takes visitors around the main landmarks surrounding the remarkable ship's history. The *Titanic* Belfast Visitor Centre encompasses nine linked interpretive galleries that recount the *Titanic*'s tale and look at Belfast's seafaring heritage in general. The stunning six-storey building, on the spot where the ship was built, has a bow-shaped facade to resemble the great vessel itself. Also on the trail are a reconstructed ship's bow, the drawing offices where the *Titanic* was conceived and the *Titanic* Dock and Pump House which make it possible to picture the sheer size of the ship – all 882 feet 9 inches of it.

BEALTAINE

Bealtaine *(Be-owl-tenna)* or May Day celebrates the arrival of summer in the early Irish calendar and is linked to abundance and growth. Pre-Christian traditions such as putting up and decorating a May bush and lighting bonfires were common elements of the annual celebration. Prayers, holy water and charms were used to keep those supernatural forces at bay that were thought to be responsible for butter, crops and cattle going missing around Bealtaine. The boundaries between the worlds of mortals and immortals blur on May Eve and it was said contact between the two was common.

If you buy what you don't
need you might have
to sell what you do.

PROVERB

POWERSCOURT HOUSE AND GARDENS

A short drive south of Dublin will bring you to the grand Powerscourt House and Gardens in County Wicklow. Comprising some 14,000 acres, the estate and gardens were built in the Palladian style in the 1730s. Sadly, due to an awful fire in 1974 much of the house was closed to the public, but the gardens and 400-foot waterfall certainly make the visit worthwhile. The grounds are a joy to explore with the nearby Sugar Loaf Mountain providing a dramatic backdrop. Terraces and walkways will lead you around picturesque features such as antique sculptures, a pond and fountain and Japanese gardens.

CLONMACNOISE MONASTERY

Clonmacnoise Monastery, Ireland's principle monastic settlement, was founded by St Ciarán between 543 and 549 CE in County Offaly. The monastery went through its greatest period of growth between the eighth and twelfth centuries when it also had to fend off numerous attacks from Vikings, Normans and even the locals. The buildings and ruins that remain include several small churches, a round tower and a small cathedral where the kings of Connacht and Tara and the last High King of Ireland, Rory O'Connor, are buried. The monastery's name is derived from the Irish *Cluain Mhic Nóis (Cluean Vic Nish)* or 'Meadow of the Sons of Nós'.

IS MAITH AN T-ANLANN AN T-OCRAS.

(Iss mah on ton-lenn on tuck-rass.)
Hunger is a good sauce.

ACHILL ISLAND

Ireland has hundreds of islands, although it is not always clear where the definition of a rock ends and that of an island begins. This is certainly not the case of Achill Island off the coast of Mayo. At 57 square miles and with a population of 2,700, it is the country's largest island. The Atlantic Drive shows off Achill's spectacular scenery, varying from hidden beaches and lakes to sheer cliff drops and soaring mountains. A deserted village of eighty stone cottages gives a glimpse at what life was like in the past. It is believed that early human settlements were established on Achill around 3000 BCE.

THE LEGEND OF OISÍN AND NIAMH

The son of Fionn mac Cumhaill and Sadbh known as Oisín *(Ush-ing)*, meaning 'little deer' wished to get to a Tír na nÓg but required a guide. This guide was Niamh Chinn Óir *(Neeve Khinn Oar)* or Niamh of the Golden Hair, the love of his life. They travel to Tír na nÓg on a magical horse that can gallop on water. One year later Oisín becomes homesick. In that time, however, 300 years have passed in his homeland. Niamh warns that when his feet touch the ground he will no longer be able to return to Tír na nÓg. While still atop the magical horse, Oisín lifts and throws a huge boulder with one hand but, alas, he falls and ages 300 years in a split second.

You'll never plough
a field by turning it
over in your mind.

PROVERB

BIRR CASTLE

Stargazers will enjoy a trip to Birr Castle, County Offaly where the Leviathan telescope is housed. The third Earl of Rosse designed and built the telescope in the 1840s and with it made some important discoveries such as the spiral character of galaxies. The Leviathan was the largest reflecting telescope in the world for more than seventy years and attracted astronomers, mathematicians and physicists from far and wide. The present castle was built in the seventeenth century on the site of a twelfth-century Norman castle. The vast castle grounds are known for their landscaped gardens and collection of exotic trees and plants.

THE LAND OF MANY NAMES

The modern Irish name for the country, Éire *(Air-ra)*, has its origins in the word Ériu *(Ai-ru)* the name of the goddess of Ireland. Éire is used to denote the country on postage stamps, coins, passports and the Irish presidential seal demonstrating citizens' pride in their ancient language and customs. Other permutations of Éire such as Erin and Éireann *(Air-ann)* are the result of the complex Gaelic grammar system. The English name for Ireland is derived from a combination of Ériu and the Germanic word 'land'. The name Hibernia was given to the island by the Roman Empire based on Ptolemy's book *Geographia* (*c.* 150 CE) where the country is referred to as Iouernía.

There are no strangers here;
only friends you
haven't yet met.

W. B. YEATS

THE BODHRÁN

At a traditional music evening in one of Ireland's many great pubs, you may notice the nation's very own percussion instrument, the bodhrán *(bow-rawn)* drum. To make the drum, cured goatskin is stretched over one side of a circular wooden frame and is often decorated with traditional Irish symbols and designs. The drum is struck with the hand or a stick known as a cipín *(kip-een)* or a tipper. The bodhrán is said to have evolved from the tambourine in the mid-twentieth century. Originally associated with the annual Wren Boy ritual on 26 December, since the revival in Irish traditional music in the 1960s and 1970s the bodhrán is a staple instrument in any 'trad' session.

THE PLAYHOUSE

In 1992, theatre-lover and costume designer Pauline Ross was at her wits' end: she had the skills to create great art, but there was no theatre space in the city. Ross managed to get a grant of £300 and opened The Playhouse in Derry/Londonderry, with a single remit: make the arts accessible to all. The intervening decades have seen it grow to become one of Ireland's leading multidisciplinary cultural and artistic institutions, with a 176-seat theatre, a dance centre and a world-leading, diverse programme of arts. It also offers training days and has inspired other creative entrepreneurs in the city.

May your home always
be too small to hold
all your friends.

TRADITIONAL IRISH TOAST

ARDMORE

Originally built as watchtowers and belfries by Christian monks, the obelisk-like round towers at Ardmore later became hiding places for monks and their valuables during Viking raids. As the entranceways are some 15 feet above the ground, monks could haul ladders into the tower after them. An excellently preserved round tower, one of the seventy remaining around the country, is one reason to visit this seaside village in County Waterford. Here you will also find the ruined twelfth-century cathedral of St Declan, compete with pillar stones with Ogham inscriptions, and the beautiful Ballyquin Beach.

BLASKET ISLANDS

Looking out to the Atlantic from the Dingle Peninsula you can see an archipelago called the Blasket Islands. One of the six islands, Tiaracht *(Teer-acht)*, is the most westerly point in Ireland and Europe. The largest of the islands, An Blascaod Mór *(On Blas-cade Moor)* or Great Blasket Island, was home to 176 people in 1916 but as there were no services on the island, inhabitants frequently had to visit the mainland. The population dwindled as many emigrated to America and the island was officially evacuated in 1953. The island produced much literature in the form of autobiographies describing vibrant island life such as that of Peig Sayers, one of Ireland's great storytellers.

Conversation may be compared to a lyre with seven chords – philosophy, art, poetry, love, scandal and the weather.

ANNA BROWNELL JAMESON

PHOENIX PARK

To escape the clogged city centre streets, one may head west along Dublin's north quays to the 1,750-acre Phoenix Park, one of Europe's largest city parks. The vast park combines formal landscaping with casual meadows and flat, open expanses with sloping, forested hillsides. As well as being home to Dublin Zoo, herds of deer freely roam the entire park. The official residence of the Irish president, the Palladian lodge Aras an Uachtarain *(Or-us an Oochk-tar-awn,)* meaning Office of the President, is also within the park. A popular jogging and cycling spot for Dubliners, the park is featured in James Joyce's *Finnegan's Wake* and other works.

THE SALMON OF KNOWLEDGE

The Salmon of Knowledge features in many tales of the Fenian Cycle of Irish mythology. By eating nine hazelnuts that fell into the Well of Wisdom from nine surrounding trees the salmon gained all the knowledge in the world. Fionn mac Cumhaill was given the salmon by a poet who had spent seven years fishing for it. Disobeying instructions, Fionn cooked the fish and burnt his thumb on it while checking if it was cooked. He sucked his thumb to reduce the pain and inadvertently received the salmon's wisdom. For the rest of his life Fionn merely had to bite his thumb to access the salmon's deep knowledge and wisdom.

Patience cures many
an old complaint.

PROVERB

GLENDALOUGH

A Wicklow gem of serene beauty is Glendalough, derived from the Irish Gleann dá Loch *(Glown daw lock)* meaning 'valley of the two lakes'. The tranquil spot is one of Ireland's main monastic sites. Located in the Wicklow Mountains National Park, the area offers many scenic walking trails such as the Wicklow Way. At Glendalough trails lead from the lower to the upper lake and around the remains of the monastery. Visitors will find a perfectly preserved eleventh- or twelfth-century round tower in a large graveyard, a seventh- to ninth-century cathedral and St Kevin's bed, a cave where the monastery founder lived as a hermit until his death in 618 CE.

TULLYNALLY CASTLE AND GARDENS

Home to the Pakenham family for over 350 years, this storybook-style castle has seen ten generations of this interesting and well-known family pass through. Originally built as a fortified house in the seventeenth century it was later converted into a Georgian mansion and transformed again in Gothic Revival style in the 1800s. The rambling castle, almost a quarter of a mile in circumference, appears a rather random collection of turrets, towers and crenulations. The rolling parkland surrounding the castle provides nearly 12 acres to explore. For wonderful views of the romantic castle take the forest path around the perimeter of the grounds.

Ever tried. Ever failed.
No matter. Try again.
Fail again. Fail better.

SAMUEL BECKETT

MULTI-PURPOSE PUBS

Not always simply a place for a drink and live music in Ireland, pubs traditionally provided a variety of goods and services for the local community. Two good examples of this still in existence are Morrissey's in Abbeyleix, Laois and McCarthy's of Fethard, Tipperary. Morrissey's shelves are lined with boxes of tea, jars of sweets, antique biscuit tins and an array of other items that are on offer in this characterful half pub, half shop. Atmospheric McCarthy's is a cosy mix of wooden booths, tables laden with pottery and trinkets from as far back as 1840. As well as serving drinks behind the bar, the establishment also functions as a restaurant and an undertaker's premises and was previously also a draper's, grocer's, china shop and more!

LÚNASA

Lúnasa *(Loo-nessa)* is the Irish name for the month of August and comes from a Gaelic festival held at the beginning of the harvest. The word 'Lúnasa' combines the name of the Celtic god Lugh *(Loo)* and the Irish word 'násad' *(naw-sad)* meaning 'assembly'. Lugh is said to have started the Lúnasa festival as a funeral feast and games to commemorate his mother Tailtiu *(Tawl-too)*. Legend claims Tailtiu died of exhaustion after she cleared the plains of Ireland for farming. Events at the Lúnasa festival included athletic and sporting contests, trading and drawing up agreements and matchmaking. Nowadays many Lúnasa fairs and festivals take place up and down the country as well as religious pilgrimages to mark the festivities at the beginning of August.

IS FEARR AN TSLÁINTE NÁ NA TÁINTE.

(Iss fahr an tlawn-tje naw na tawn-tje.)
Health is better than wealth.

VIKING CEMETERIES

Furnished graves uncovered between 1846 and 1934 in the areas of Islandbridge and Kilmainham in Dublin provide the strongest archaeological evidence of the Viking period in their history of Ireland. The findings in these sites represent the largest collection of Viking grave goods outside Scandanavia. Males were typically buried with swords, spears and shields, and females with oval brooches and other jewellery or ornaments. Both cremation and burial were practised within a century of 841 CE, when Dublin was founded. The Viking Ireland exhibition at the National Museum of Ireland displays findings from cemetery excavations, and visitors to Dublinia *(Dove-linia)* heritage centre can explore the Viking times through interactive exhibitions.

THE MOURNE MOUNTAINS

Hikers and walkers could never be disappointed with the trails and the lovely people of the Mourne Mountains. These mountains, the tallest in Ireland, are granite, rising up against the Irish Sea, and just a stone's throw from the fishing of Strangford Lough. C. S. Lewis hid in a wardrobe as a child in east Belfast and imagined travelling back to those rugged mountains. The intrepid walker would be well-served by the local ales brewed in south Down, and refreshed and fortified by langoustines and oysters on offer in the seaside town of Dundrum.

The ocean is a central image. It is the symbolism of a great journey.

ENYA

DEIRDRE

Also referred to as 'Deirdre of the Sorrows', one of Irish mythology's best-known characters is also its leading tragic hero. Before she was born it was foretold that Deirdre *(Deer-dra)* would cause trouble and bloodshed. Upon spying a raven in the snow drinking the blood of a slaughtered animal Deidre decided her husband should have white skin, red cheeks and black hair. She fell in love and eloped with Naoise *(Knee-shah)* who fit the description, despite having been selected by a king who wanted Deidre to become his wife. The king invited the couple back to Ireland but Naoise is killed for treachery and Deirdre is taken. Deirdre, in protest, jumps from a moving chariot and her head is shattered in the fall.

WESTERN LANDSCAPES

In the far west of Ireland lies an enchanting, rugged landscape where misty bogland meets heather-clad hilltops and sparkling blue lakes are never far from sight. Counties Galway and Mayo are perfect for hikers seeking unspoilt countryside and peace. For those in need of a little space, Connemara National Park in Galway offers 5,000 acres of wilderness around the Twelve Bens mountain range. The 30-mile Galway Western Way hiking trail covers places of striking beauty such as Loch Corrib – Ireland's second largest lake – and its only fjord at Killary Harbour. From Killary Harbour you can continue on the Mayo Western Way, another 110 miles of dramatic countryside.

And there's the half-talk
code of mysteries
And the wink-and-elbow
language of delight.

PATRICK KAVANAGH

THE MANY NAMES OF DUBLIN

The origins of the word Dublin can confuse even Dubliners themselves as it bears no resemblance to its Irish name. This is because the city's Irish and English names have different roots. The Irish name, Baile Atha Cliath *(Boll-ya Awe-ha Klia)* means 'Town of the Hurdle Fort', reflecting a prehistoric hurdlework feature that made the Liffey passable. A 'dark pool' in the River Poddle is the origin of the name Dubhlinn *(Dove-lin)*. When Norse Vikings settled in Dublin in 841 CE the town's name became Dyfflin and its surrounding territory Dyflinnarskíri (Dublinshire). The city's early English name was Divelinn, which gradually became Dublin.

TRINITY COLLEGE LIBRARY

Ireland's largest and arguably most beautiful library is located in Trinity College, Dublin. It was established along with the college in 1592 and contains five million printed volumes including a broad range of manuscripts, journals, music and maps from the last 400 years. Hundreds of thousands of visitors come to the old library each year to explore its rich collection and exhibitions. The library's most famous manuscripts are the *Book of Kells* and the *Book of Durrow*, illuminated manuscripts in a very ornate style created *c.* 800 CE and *c.* 700 CE.

Ireland is a great country
to die or be married in.

ELIZABETH BOWEN

CARRICK-A-REDE ROPE BRIDGE

Every year hundreds of thousands of visitors risk life and limb to cross the 66-foot-long rope bridge to the tiny island of Carrick-a-Rede near Ballintoy, County Antrim. Although the bridge is not actually as dangerous as it initially seems, the various forms it has taken in over 350 years of existence may not all have been for the faint-hearted. Even today tourists take fright and choose to return to the mainland by boat rather than cross the bridge again. Those up for the challenge are rewarded with beautiful scenic views while the rope swings to the tune of the crashing waves 98 feet below.

NATIONAL PLOUGHING CHAMPIONSHIPS

In 1931 two friends, one from County Wexford and the other County Kildare, had an argument about which county had the best ploughmen. The men set a challenge and so began Ireland's National Ploughing Championships. Every September the event attracts up to 190,000 visitors to watch over 330 ploughing competitors compete during the three days. The event is no longer just about ploughing however, visitors also come for the craft village, food fairs, fashion shows and sheepdog trials and even the all-Ireland lamb shearing in this annual celebration of Irish food, farming and culture.

May you live as long as
you want and never want
as long as you live.

TRADITIONAL IRISH TOAST

BLOOMSDAY

Leopold Bloom, the protagonist in James Joyce's *Ulysses*, spent 16 June 1904 walking around Dublin into the wee hours. The novel chronicles this ordinary day in Bloom's life and the characters he encounters on his Dublin odyssey. The date was chosen as it matched the day Joyce went on the first date with his wife-to-be Nora Barnacle. Nowadays if you walk around Dublin on 16 June don't be surprised if you come across some interesting characters in Edwardian clothing, retracing Bloom's steps and acting out scenes from the book. Dubliners celebrate 'Bloomsday' annually with a host of cultural and literary events.

CEOL AGUS CRAIC

Ceol agus craic *(key-ole ahgus crack)* are key to leisure time in Ireland. Roughly meaning music and merriment, you will experience it first-hand at the many traditional pubs around the country. Second only to the people and the atmosphere, the instruments play an essential role in 'trad' music sessions. As well as the bodhrán, you'll commonly see a tin whistle – a metallic tube with a mouthpiece and six holes – as well as a flute and accordion. A fiddle, which only differs from a violin in name, and uilleann pipes, similar to bagpipes, will normally also feature for a rich, round sound.

Always forgive your enemies; nothing annoys them so much.

OSCAR WILDE

WEST CORK

The historic old port town known as the gourmet capital of Ireland, Kinsale, is an ideal spot to commence the 85-mile drive around scenic west Cork. The trip will take you to green Glengariff via Bantry Bay. An area replete with idyllic beaches, rugged peninsulas and picturesque towns, it's best to travel around at your leisure with plenty of stop-offs. Colourful Clonakilty definitely deserves a visit, as does Bantry House and Gardens and the romantic island gardens of Ilnacullin to name but a handful of must-see places along the way.

THE CHILDREN OF LIR

The tragic story of the Children of Lir is a classic Irish folk tale from the fifteenth century. It recounts the story of the jealousy Aoife *(Ee-fa)* feels towards her new husband Chieftan Lir's children from a previous marriage, causing her to decide to turn them into swans. The children spend 900 unhappy years as swans before being finally allowed to return home. Home is now deserted so they travel to Inishglora off the coast of County Mayo where a holy man treats them kindly. The children become human again but are extremely old so the holy man baptises them and they sadly die.

A friend's eye is a
good mirror.

PROVERB

IRISH STOUT

Irish stout is famous for its dark black colour, creamy texture and long-lasting head. It is also known for having to be poured in a curious fashion to get that perfect texture and flavour. The best-known Irish stout around the world would probably be the Dublin-brewed Guinness. At home on the Emerald Isle however, Cork-brewed Murphy's and Beamish are tasty treats that make for some tough competition. Also, in recent years other brewpubs and microbreweries have emerged, offering delights such as flavourful Porterhouse Oyster Stout, O'Hara's Celtic Stout and Mourne Oyster Stout, providing a richer Irish stout experience.

DUBLIN LITERARY PUB CRAWL

Since the late 1980s this immensely popular tour has provided Dubliners and tourists alike with alternative insight into the Dublin literary hall of fame. Charismatic actors lead a group around some of the city's favourite pubs and historic spots on an entertaining journey through Dublin literary history. While soaking up the atmosphere of the city at night and its fine drinking establishments, participants are treated to renditions of prose, song and drama, along with historical facts about the city itself. Literary giants such as Joyce, Behan, O'Casey and Shaw all feature among others as the pub crawl makes its way through the city streets – starting each evening at the Duke, a pub frequented by many of Ireland's writing legends.

IS MAITH AN SCÉALAÍ AN AIMSIR.

(Iss mah on shkay-ly on I'm-sure.)
Time is a good storyteller.

THE BOGLANDS

On a cold winter's evening the smoky scent wafting from chimneys across the Emerald Isle emanates from peat burning in the household hearth. The country's many chocolate-brown boglands are the source of this fuel. While once almost 20 per cent of the country was covered by bogs, nowadays it is sadly closer to 2 per cent. The bogs are home to a broad range of wildlife – such as white-fronted geese, butterflies, larks and an extensive variety of frogs – and are an important source of prehistoric, archaeological finds. The Bog of Allen, Ireland's best-known bog, stretches across nine counties in the midlands.

TRADITIONAL GAMES

Ireland has several indigenous sports played at home and abroad. Stick-and-ball games, camogie (for women) and hurling (for men), are very fast-moving and require much skill. They have been played for several thousand years and share a common Gaelic root with shinty, mainly played in Scotland. The games take place on pitches approximately 450 feet long and 270 feet wide, where fifteen players on each team aim to get points by striking the ball, called a sliotar *(schlit-or)*, under or over the bar of the H-shaped goals. The wooden stick used is called a camán *(cam-on)* or hurley. It curves outwards at the end and is usually made from ash.

If you get a reputation
as an early riser, you
can sleep till noon.

PROVERB

DUBLIN ART MUSEUMS

The IMMA or Irish Museum of Modern Art is housed in the late-seventeenth-century Royal Hospital in Kilmainham, Dublin. The museum contains several important collections of twentieth-century Irish and international art, including works by Jack B. Yeats and Louis le Brocquy. The grounds also make a pleasant spot for a walk or to sit and relax in what was originally built as a hospice for retired soldiers. Art lovers should also visit the National Gallery on Merrion Square, Dublin for an interesting collection of Irish and European fine art as well as excellent temporary exhibitions. In Temple Bar the top-notch gallery is sure to satisfy the keenest of photography aficionados.

THE BURREN

Despite Ireland's fame as 'the Emerald Isle', full of green pastures and forests, the area known as the Burren in counties Clare and Galway tells a different story. For some 160 square miles the traditional forty shades of green becomes a starker grey and brown landscape of limestone rock formulated over millennia. Contrary to its lifeless appearance, a ramble will reveal the Burren is host to a rich variety of flora and fauna, 'disappearing lakes' and dense cave networks. A myriad of archaeological sites such as 4,000-year-old tombs, dolmens (tombs consisting of several standing stones supporting a horizontal stone) and stone forts can be found in the rocky terrain, which supports 70 per cent of Ireland's native wildflower species, despite making up only 1 per cent of its land mass.

There's kind of a calling in
Irish voices when they're
singing in their Irish accent.

SINÉAD O'CONNOR

THE YEATS TRAIL

The famous poet and playwright William Butler Yeats (1865–1939) had a strong connection to County Sligo and took inspiration in its dramatic landscape, mythology and folklore. He was buried here according to his wishes in the place he called 'the country of the heart'. The Yeats Trail will take you around the places closely related to W. B. Yeats in Dublin, Galway and most of all Sligo. 'Places of silence and solitude' frequented by Yeats form part of the trail such as the waterfall in Glencar, rugged Dooney Rock as well as Drumcliff church and graveyard where Yeats is buried.

KING JOHN'S CASTLE

Take a stroll along the west bank of the River Shannon in Limerick city for the best views of King John's Castle. The castle was built in 1200 CE on a Viking site, dating from 922 CE, by King John of England on the site of earlier Norman fortifications and was the administrative and military centre for the Shannon area. Inside the castle the history of Limerick and Ireland is brought to life in an audio-visual show, brutal medieval weapons are recreated and the archaeology centre displays Viking and Norman features and artefacts. Climbing the drum tower in the oldest section of the castle affords great views of the city and the Shannon.

Remember even if you lose all, keep your good name; for if you lose that you are worthless.

PROVERB

PLACE NAMES IN IRELAND

Place names in Ireland are confusing at the best of times, even to the locals. They can be long, with complicated spelling and even more complicated pronunciation, but are nonetheless beautiful. The confusion arose because most of the names were originally in the Irish language and later adapted to English phonology and spelling. Historically, towns and settlements in Ireland were small and so places were named after features in the landscape such as lakes, rocks and hills; later names were taken from man-made features such as castles and bridges. A few examples are: 'bally' from the Irish *baile* meaning 'settlement', 'dun' from the Irish *dún* meaning 'fort' and 'kil' from *cill* or 'church'. This can lead to place names such as Muiceanach idir Dhá Sháile *(Mwik-enoch idr gaw hall-ya)* literally, 'Pig-marsh between Two Saltwaters'.

BOGSIDE MURALS

Twelve murals decorate the houses along Rossville Street in the area of Derry/Londonderry called Bogside, to the west of the walled city. The murals, known collectively as the People's Gallery, commemorate key events from the period of the Troubles. The Bogside artists who painted the murals between 1997 and 2001 are two brothers and a friend who grew up in the area and experienced the worst of the Troubles. Bogside was developed in the nineteenth and early twentieth centuries as a working-class residential area that was predominantly Catholic. It has seen much redevelopment in recent years with modern housing replacing the old dwellings.

There is no love sincerer than the love of food.

GEORGE BERNARD SHAW

THE ARAN ISLANDS

Inishmore (12 square miles), Inishmaan (3½ square miles) and Inisheer (2¼ square miles) make up the Aran Islands off the west coast. The landscape across all three islands is known for its small fields enclosed by dry-stone walling. The islands are famous for Aran knitting with its intricate stitching patterns inspired by life on the islands, resulting in names like cable, blackberry and diamond. Numerous stone forts, presumed to be from the late Bronze Age, can be found on the islands as well as early Christian architectural remains.

AISLINGE

Aislinge *(Ash-ling)* is an early style of Irish prose which generically involves a hero who has a vision or dream. One of the most well-known tales of this genre is the 'Aislinge Óenguso' *(Ash-ling-eh Ain-goso)*, 'The dream of Óengus'. Óengus falls in love with a beautiful woman evoked in a dream. The woman, who goes by the name of Cáer, is the daughter of the King of the Connacht. Cáer alternates her form between human and swan. The lovers meet, become swans and fly off together there. W. B. Yeats's poem 'The Song of Wandering Aengus' takes its inspiration from this tale.

Say little, but say it well.

PROVERB

WESTPORT

The colourful town of Westport, in County Mayo, is an eighteenth-century Georgian-style heritage town. The tree-lined streets are full of top-quality restaurants and vibrant pubs. It is set on Clew Bay inlet, a lovely spot at sundown to look out to the hundreds of little islands dotting the sea. The largest is Clare Island which sits at the mouth of the bay and affords wonderful views south to Connemara and north to Achill Island. The 2,500-foot-high Croagh Patrick, distinctively conical in shape, towers over the bay. St Patrick reputedly spent forty days and nights of Lent fasting here in 441 CE when converting Ireland to Christianity.

SAMHAIN

Samhain *(Sau-wan)* is a Gaelic festival celebrated from sunset on 31 October to sunset on 1 November. It is also the Irish word for the month of November. It marks the end of the harvest season and the start of winter, at which time cattle are returned from summer pastures and livestock slaughtered. Traditionally bonfires were lit and as a cleansing ritual people and their livestock walked between two fires. There was contact with the 'otherworld' beyond the land of the living, and the souls of the dead were called to attend feasts where places were set for them.

AN TÉ A THABHARFAS SCÉAL CHUGAT TABHARFAIDH SÉ DHÁ SCÉAL UAIT.

(On tay a her-fas shkay-al hug-at ter-fig shkay-al gaw skay-al oo-at.)
Whoever comes to you with a story will bring two away from you.

GLENCOLUMBKILLE

Glencolumbkille *(Glen-colum-killa),* from the Irish Gleann Cholm Cille, is a tiny remote hamlet at the heart of the Gaeltacht area of Donegal and takes its name from St Columba, the Christian missionary who lived here during the sixth century. Cliffs up to 700 feet high surround this brightly painted village, many dotted with ancient hermit cells from the monastery established here by St Columba. The area has been inhabited since 3000 BCE and contains Stone Age remains such as a ring fort and burial cairns. St Columba allegedly inscribed forty prehistoric standing stones with the sign of the cross to incorporate the stones into Christian usage.

CÚPLA FOCAL

Knowing 'cúpla focal' (*coop-lah fuk-le* – a few words) 'as Gaelige' *(oss Gwail-iga* – in Irish) will certainly go down well with the locals. Try starting with 'Dia dhuit' (*Dee-ya gwhich)* or hello, which taken more literally means 'God be with you'. The reply is 'Dia is Muire dhuit' *(Dee-ya iss Mwir-a gwhich)* or 'God and Mary be with you'. 'Conas atá tú?' *(Kunnas a-taw too)* or 'How are you?' is normally replied to with 'Táim go maith' *(Tawm gu mah)* or 'I'm well'. For 'thank you' try 'Go raibh maith agat' *(Gu rev mah agut)* to which you'll hear 'Tá fáilte romhat' *(Tah foil-tya row-at)* or 'You're welcome'.

There is no such thing
as bad publicity, except
your own obituary.

BRENDAN BEHAN

ATHLONE TOWN

Midway on your journey between Dublin and Galway, you'll find Athlone in County Westmeath. Split in two by the River Shannon, the thriving town has undergone significant regeneration. The western bank's winding, colourful streets, full of interesting little shops and excellent restaurants, are overlooked by the well-preserved twelfth-century Athlone Castle. Here you will also find Sean's Bar, Ireland's (and possibly the world's!) oldest pub, dating back to 900 CE, complete with sawdust on the floor, low ceilings, display cases full of all sorts of oddities and most likely a few musicians playing in the corner.

TED FEST

Each February since 2007, fans and fanatics of the sitcom *Father Ted* spend a few rather quirky days at an annual convention known as Friends of Ted Festival or 'Ted Fest'. Following in the footsteps of the television series, Ted Fest takes place on an island off the west coast. Inishmore, the largest of the Aran islands, plays host to the motley crew who descend upon it dressed as priests, nuns or other characters from the show. Everyone gets a little silly for a few days and takes part in games and competitions based on scenes and themes from their favourite comedy series.

If you're lucky enough
to be Irish, then you're
lucky enough.

ANONYMOUS

CÉIDE FIELDS

One day in the 1930s while cutting turf for fuel, Patrick Caulfield came across piles of stones beneath the bog and so the world's most extensive Stone Age site was discovered in Mayo. Patrick's son, Seamus, went on to study archaeology and thoroughly investigated the area forty years later. Excavations revealed megalithic tombs, stone-walled fields and houses all approximately 5,500 years old, older than both the Pyramid at Giza and Stonehenge. The award-winning interpretive centre provides fascinating insight into the Céide *(Kay-dja)* Fields complex back then. The area is also known for its superb coastal scenery, with beautiful beaches and dramatic cliffs.

ST COLUMB'S CATHEDRAL

Named for St Columba, the missionary who left Ireland to bring Christianity to Scotland and the north of England, St Columb's is the 'mother church' for the Church of Ireland, being the first cathedral built after the Protestant Reformation in the British Isles. It lends the distinctive shape of its spire to all Protestant churches throughout Ireland. Despite its status as a Protestant church, St Columb's was a centre of inter-community activities throughout the Troubles – including religious and secular activities. It holds many documents relating to the Siege of Derry as well as a chalice given to the church by James I (James VI in Scotland) in 1613, which is still used for special communion ceremonies.

Your feet will take you
where your heart is.

PROVERB

THE HARP

The history of the Irish harp dates back at least 1,000 years. In medieval times, harpists were in demand across Ireland and were among the most important of musicians. Kings and chieftains employed a resident harpist to accompany the singing of psalms and poetry recitals. The Irish harp is unique in having a resonating chamber carved from a single willow log, as opposed to being constructed of several pieces, and in utilising brass strings. It can be found on early Christian stone crosses and manuscripts, on Irish coins minted by Henry VIII, and continues to be emblematic of Ireland, being found on passports, official documents, Irish Euro coins and the presidential seal.

TRIM

This quiet, unassuming town in County Meath, known in Irish as Baile Átha Troim *(Boll-ya Awe-ha Trim)*, or 'Town of the Elderflowers', is dotted with remnants of its historic importance. Originally sited at a monastery most likely founded by St Patrick, it grew into a walled city of strategic importance at the edge of the Anglo-Norman Pale region. Trim was also a centre for culture, including no fewer than seven monasteries and Elizabeth I's planned site for the university that became Trinity College, Dublin. Tiny old workers' cottages line the streets and you'll find ruins all around the town. Thin Lizzy and U2 both had early concerts here, and Trim Castle was used as a location in the film *Braveheart* (1995).

Our Irish blunders are never blunders of the heart.

MARIA EDGEWORTH

IRISH WHISKEY

The Gaelic term 'uisce beatha' *(ish-ka ba-ha)* meaning 'water of life' is the origin of the word 'whiskey'. Irish whiskey is said to be one of the earliest drinks distilled in Europe; twelfth-century Irish monks brought the technique of distilling perfume from the Mediterranean – later modified to produce the celebrated spirit. Irish whiskeys are aged for a minimum of three years in wooden barrels, though almost none should be drunk that young. Samuel Johnson's entry for whiskey in his 1755 dictionary read 'the Irish sort is particularly distinguished for its pleasant and mild flavour' – this due to the triple distillation that lends smoothness to this spirit enjoyed around the world.

MUSEUM OF COUNTRY LIFE

A reminder of bygone days, this branch of the National Museum of Ireland, which sees around a million visitors a year, will take you back to rural Ireland between 1860 and 1960. This is a time before rural electrification, when fires were lit for heating and cooking, water was carried from a well and turf brought home from the bog. In contrast, the restored rooms of Turlough Park House give insight into the lifestyle of the landowners. Exhibits include original clothing, utensils, furniture and agricultural implements. Temporary exhibitions highlight differences between then and now and compare romanticised impressions of times gone by with the harsh realities experienced by those at the time.

May you have a song in
your heart, a smile on
your lips and nothing but
joy at your fingertips!

TRADITIONAL IRISH TOAST

LISMORE

Set on the banks of the River Blackwater, the elegant and enchanting town of Lismore in Waterford attracts historians and anglers alike. The enormous (*lis* is Irish for 'fort', and '*mór*' means 'big') castle was built in the nineteenth century on a site with a colourful history dating back to a monastery here in the seventh century. It makes a striking sight upon crossing the river into the town. The gardens offer pleasant woodland walks or one can embark on the intriguing yew walk, reputedly more than 800 years old. The town is also home to two cathedrals and during its time as an important monastic centre between the seventh and twelfth centuries, a highly regarded university was located here. Hit badly by the great famine in 1845, the famine graveyard is a poignant reminder of that tragic time.

IMBOLC

To mark the start of spring, Imbolc *(I-molk)* was celebrated in Celtic Ireland from 31 January to 1 February. Imbolc comes from the Irish 'i mbolg' *(i molg)* meaning 'in the belly', referring to the pregnancy of ewes. This pagan festival was originally associated with the goddess Brighid *(Bre-gid)*, who is said to visit and bring luck to households on Imbolc eve. People would leave food and drink for Brighid and make a bed for her. These rituals were Christianised and the first of February named St Brighid's Day. Brighid's crosses made from rushes are hung over doors, windows and stables to invite Brighid to bless and protect the buildings.

TÚS MAITH LEATH NA HOIBRE.

(Too-ss mah lah na hib-ra.)
A good start halves the work.

RATHCROGAN

Meaning the 'Ringfort of Cruachan', this complex of over fifty archaeological monuments in Roscommon was of great significance in ancient times as a place of burial and ritual gatherings. Cruachan is the original capital of Connacht and much of the Ulster Cycle of literature is centred around the area. Tales recount the life of Queen Maeve or Meabh *(Mave)*, the goddess of sovereignty who ruled Connacht. The site is strongly linked with the Gaelic festival of Samhain *(Sau-wan)* when there was contact with those beyond the grave. The mysterious natural stone cave – Cave of the Cats – can be found at Rathcrogan, an important entranceway to the 'otherworld' since the Bronze Age.

THE GIANT'S CAUSEWAY

Legend has it that this extraordinary feature on the Antrim coast was created by the giant Fionn mac Cumhaill to enable him to fight with his Scottish opponent, the giant Benandonner. There are further signs of giant activity nearby, including the rock formations known as the Giant's Boot and the Wishing Chair. It is, in fact, the result of volcanic activity some 50 to 60 million years ago and the remarkable polygonal shapes, which interlock like jigsaw pieces, were formed by the rapid cooling of lava – some of the pillars are over 39 feet high!

If you do not sow in the spring you will not reap in the autumn.

PROVERB

IRISH DANCING

Irish dancing can be performed solo, in an organised group or can be a more social affair. Solo dances include reels, jigs and hornpipes which were brought to the country by travelling dance masters during the eighteenth and nineteenth centuries and feature in competitive dancing. They can be performed in soft or hard shoes. When dancing in soft shoes, the graceful, airborne nature of the dance is emphasised, while hard shoes beat out the rhythm and accompany the music. Social dances can be set dances where four couples dance arranged in a square, or céilí *(kay-lee)* dances that are various formations of two to sixteen people.

SYMBOLS OF IRELAND

How did it come about that shamrocks and Celtic crosses typically symbolise Ireland? It seems St Patrick used the shamrock to illustrate the doctrine of the Holy Trinity when he was Christianising Ireland. As St Patrick is the patron saint of Ireland, the shamrock was chosen to represent the country in the eighteenth century and is worn on lapels on St Patrick's Day. Lore surrounding the Celtic cross suggests that St Patrick tried to entice pagan followers by combining their worship of the sun with that of the cross. The mid-nineteenth century Celtic Revival resulted in the cross being used to represent a sense of heritage in Ireland.

To create, one must first question everything.

EILEEN GRAY

DERRY/LONDONDERRY CITY WALLS

The finest example of intact city walls in Europe surround and protect Derry/Londonderry. Built between 1614 and 1618 the mile-long walls were originally constructed with four gates, with three more added in the eighteenth and nineteenth centuries. A stroll along the rampart walkway is the best way to appreciate the 400-year-old walls and get a living sense of Derry/Londonderry's thousand years of history from St Columb's voyage right up through modern times. The ramparts are often also the best way to get where you're going! The Tower Museum, the oldest structure in Derry/Londonderry, and St Columb's Cathedral are nearby.

CARRAUNTOOHIL

Along the Hag's Glen and up the Devil's Ladder the route to the summit of Ireland's highest peak can be found. At around 3,400 feet high climbers may be rewarded with views as far as Galway if they are lucky enough to arrive on one of those rare non-misty days. Carrauntoohil *(Karan-tu-hill)* is located in the Macgillycuddy's Reeks range, along with another five peaks that reach over 3,000 feet tall, on the Iveragh Peninsula, County Kerry. The mountain's name is derived from the Irish Corrán Tuathail *(Core-awn Toohill)* which translates as 'Tuathal's sickle'.

What is nearest the heart
is nearest the mouth.

PROVERB

THE ROCK OF CASHEL

Cashel, in the heart of County Tipperary, is home to a spectacular collection of medieval buildings called the Rock of Cashel that overlooks the town. Legend has it the rock formed when St Patrick banished the devil from a nearby cave. The devil, in anger, took a bite out of a mountain known as Devil's Bit, but broke its teeth and part of the mountain landed in Cashel. For this reason the rock is also referred to as Carraig Phádraig *(Ka-rig Fawd-rig)* or St Patrick's Rock. The Rock of Cashel was the principal seat of the kings of Munster for hundreds of years before the Normans arrived.

BELFAST PUBS

Two of Belfast's top pubs in which to while away an evening are the Crown Liquor Saloon and The John Hewitt. The opulent Crown Liquor Saloon originally opened as the Railway Tavern in 1826. Excellently preserved, it is still lighted by gas lamps and guests can get the bar person's attention using the antique push-button bells from their carved wooden snug – replete with mirrors and columns, it is the perfect example of the Victorian public house. The John Hewitt, named after one of Ulster's most famous poets, is a cosy traditional pub with high ceilings, an open fire, wooden panelling and plenty of live music.

The sound of [uilleann] pipes is a little bit of heaven to some of us.

NANCY O'KEEFE

BENBULBEN

The mysterious rock formation of Benbulben can be seen all along the northern coast of County Sligo. The 1,730-foot-tall flat-topped mountain is found in Yeats country and part of the Dartry Mountains. Its sides are almost vertical and scored by long ridges. Many Celtic legends, such as tales involving Fionn mac Cumhaill and his warriors, the Fianna, are set at Benbulben. One such tale involves Fionn convincing an opponent warrior, Diarmud *(Deer-muid)* to fight an enchanted boar which pierced Diarmud's heart with a tusk and killed him.

OMAGH

The busy market town of Omagh in County Tyrone suffered a terrible tragedy at the tail end of the Troubles which turned hearts and minds in favour of the peace process. The Garden of Light memorial is a touching reminder of the tragic bomb that devastated the town in 1998. The memorial makes creative use of mirrors and sunlight to illuminate a heart-shaped crystal in an obelisk at the actual bomb site 100 yards away. Thirty-one mirrors, one for each life lost, track the sun and reflect light down the street, where another mirror reflects it around the corner to the obelisk on Market Street. The memorial embodies the spirit of remembrance and the triumph of light over darkness.

May the road rise to
meet you, may the wind
be always at your back,
the sunshine warm upon
your face, the rainfall
soft upon your fields.

TRADITIONAL IRISH TOAST

THE RING OF KERRY

Travelling clockwise from the town of Killarney in County Kerry around the Iveragh Peninsula, travellers will experience some of the most stunning scenery Ireland has to offer. The 110-mile-long circular tourist route known as the Ring of Kerry is replete with scenic beaches, waterfalls, castles and walkways. The area is also steeped in history with many interesting archaeological sites dotted along the way, one example being a stone circle from the Bronze Age known locally as the Seven Sisters. Beehive cells in the remains of a monastic settlement can also be found, as can ancient Ogham stones.

PUCK FAIR

Every year residents of Killorgan, County Kerry, head to the mountains to find a goat to crown King Puck at one of Ireland's oldest festivals, Puck Fair. During three days in August animals are traded, and streets fill with music and dancing, craft and food stalls, fireworks and performers. Queen Puck, a local girl, clad in traditional robes and gown, crowns the goat King Puck and the festivities commence. King Puck is hoisted atop a platform where he surveys the festivities. There are many stories surrounding the origins of Puck Fair, scholars claim it is Pre-Christian and the goat is a pagan symbol of fertility in the typical harvest-time festival.

For you can't hear
Irish tunes without
knowing you're Irish,
and wanting to pound
that fact into the floor.

JENNIFER ARMSTRONG

GALWAY CITY

It's easy to feel at home in Galway city. The Anglo-Norman establishment, founded in the mid-thirteenth century, is full of life yet moves at its own laid-back pace. The city centre is a warren of winding, colourful streets full of interesting shops, great restaurants, inviting pubs and welcoming people. Cobblestones and low-rise buildings add to its small-town charm. A musical town, it is known for its street buskers and gigs and attracts creatives such as writers and theatre folk. It is no surprise then that a cultural festival is on the agenda every second weekend.

LISDOONVARNA

Each September tens of thousands of people descend upon the small town of Lisdoonvarna in County Clare in search of romance and *craic* (fun). The current matchmaker, Willie Daly, is the third generation of a family of matchmakers who have been bringing happy couples together for around 150 years. The name Lisdoonvarna comes from the Irish 'Lios Dúin Bhearna' *(Lish Doon Varna)* which means 'Enclosure at the Fort by the Gap'. The fort in question is thought to be the green earthen fort of Lissateeaun (Fort of the Fairy Hill), a few minutes' drive to the north-east of Lisdoonvarna.

There are good ships,
and there are wood ships,
the ships that sail the
sea. But the best ships,
are friendships, and
may they always be.

PROVERB

THE RIVER SHANNON

The longest river in Ireland is said to take its name from the Celtic goddess, Sionann *(She-o-nan)*. The 224-mile-long river virtually splits the country in half. Rising in County Cavan, it runs through or between eleven counties before reaching the Atlantic Ocean at the Shannon Estuary in County Limerick. An ancient Irish manuscript, the *Book of Lismore*, claims the Shannon is home to a large monster with a horse's mane and a whale's tail that goes by the name of Cata. To modern eyes, however, only the usual fish and river wildlife are visible!

GO N'ÉIRÍ AN T-ÁDH LEAT.

(Gu nigh ree on taw lath.)
May luck rise with you.

Clare Gallagher grew up in Dublin and has devoted much time to exploring the Emerald Isle and seeking out its cultural and historical treasures. A linguist at heart, she also spent time in the Gaeltacht areas perfecting her command of the Irish language while growing up. She has travelled widely and now lives in London with her partner where she works as a teacher and translator.

Just for the Craic

the very best irish jokes

Cormac O'Brien

JUST FOR THE CRAIC
The Very Best Irish Jokes

Cormac O'Brien

ISBN: 978 1 84953 351 5
£4.99
Hardback

'What would you be if you weren't
Irish?' asked the barman.
Pat replied, 'Ashamed!'

The Irish love a good laugh, even if the laugh s on them! Enjoy cover-to-cover giggles with this pocket-sized parcel packed full of the very best Irish jokes and yarns.